Basic Skil

Main Idea

Using Topics and Details to See the Big Picture

Grades 3–4

by

Jennifer Rozines Roy

Instructional Fair
An imprint of Carson-Dellosa Publishing LLC
Greensboro, North Carolina

Instructional Fair

Author: Jennifer Rozines Roy
Editors: Sara Bierling, Kathryn Wheeler, Sharon Kirkwood
Cover Artist: Sherry Neidigh
Interior Artist: Theresa Wright

Instructional Fair
An imprint of Carson-Dellosa Publishing LLC
PO Box 35665
Greensboro, NC 27425 USA

ISBN 978-1-56822-931-7
060117800

About the Book

The activities in *Main Idea* include high-interest reading selections with activities that teach and reinforce the concepts of main idea, topic, topic sentence, and supporting details. With a variety of fun and instructional formats, teachers can provide direct instruction, reinforcement, or independent practice throughout the year. When possible, lessons are linked to other curriculum areas such as math, science, social studies, and language arts. With this format, *Main Idea* also offers students the opportunity to learn and practice skills such as critical thinking, comprehension, and writing in an enjoyable and creative format. Review pages are also included to assess and reinforce student learning.

Table of Contents

Mapping the Main Idea

To find the main idea of a piece of writing, ask this question: What is the writer telling me?

Read the following paragraphs. Then, complete the exercises below.

1. When you take a trip to somewhere you have never been, it is wise to bring a map with you. Maps provide information about an area. Depending on the type of map, they show features such as roads, buildings, and bodies of water. Maps help people get to where they want to go. Maps are a very helpful tool for travelers.

What is the main idea?

    a. Maps help travelers get to where they want to go.

    b. Maps show bodies of water.

    c. Wise travelers use maps.

2. A person who makes maps is called a cartographer. A cartographer draws the features on a map. It is very important for cartographers to measure and draw carefully so that the map is accurate. It takes a lot of skill and patience to be a cartographer!

What is the main idea?

    a. Patient people make good cartographers.

    b. Cartographers must measure accurately.

    c. Cartographers are skilled people who make maps.

Do the wordsearch! Circle all the words listed in the box. Look ↑ ↓ → ← .

All of the words are things that can be found on maps.

S	E	E	R	G	E	D
J	K	A	K	A	B	I
S	A	S	R	E	G	R
O	L	T	S	E	W	E
U	R	E	V	I	R	C
T	R	O	A	D	K	T
H	T	R	O	N	E	I
R	K	C	I	T	Y	O
L	E	G	E	N	D	N

Degrees   South
Direction   West
East   Key
Legend   North
Lake   City
River   Road

What's the Main Idea?

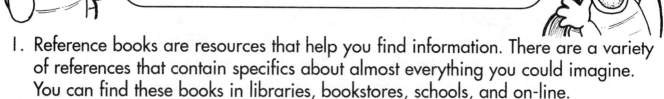

Read each of the following paragraphs. Circle the letter that tells the main idea of each paragraph.

1. Reference books are resources that help you find information. There are a variety of references that contain specifics about almost everything you could imagine. You can find these books in libraries, bookstores, schools, and on-line.

   a. Libraries are good places to find reference books.
   b. Reference books come in a variety of forms.
   c. Reference books are good resources for information.

2. An almanac is one example of a reference book. Almanacs contain facts and information about a specific year. They describe events and tally statistics. If you want to know what happened during the year you were born, refer to the almanac for that year!

   a. Almanacs contain facts and information about a specific year.
   b. Almanacs show what happened the year you were born.
   c. Almanacs include descriptions of events and statistics.

3. Another type of reference book is a thesaurus. This book contains synonyms and antonyms. For example, if you want to know another word for *thin*, you might use a thesaurus. You will find synonyms such as *skinny* and *svelte*. The thesaurus will also show some opposite words such as *heavy* and *obese*.

   a. If you want another word for *thin*, you might use a thesaurus.
   b. A thesaurus is a reference book that contains synonyms and antonyms.
   c. A synonym for *skinny* is *thin*.

> **Try this:** Look in an almanac for the year you were born! Find out interesting facts such as the number–one song, the president of the United States, and the best-selling book for that year.

  5

I Scream, You Scream!

Summer's almost here and the temp's gonna rise! So why not cool off with some refreshing, nutritious ice cream? Ice cream, you say? But of course. With Iditarod Ice Cream you get all of the vitamins found in a head of broccoli and more. Iditarod adds 100% of every vitamin and mineral to its mixture of cream and sugar. We also add all-natural flavors to make this ice cream the most refreshing and tasty. Not one preservative is added to our healthy creation. You won't regret making this positive life change!

Try some Iditarod Ice Cream today!

Comes in 40 fabulous flavors!

1. What is the main thing that makes this ice cream so special? It...

   a. has lots of vitamins.   b. contains no preservatives.

   c. comes in 40 flavors.   d. is refreshing and nutritious.

2. What examples does the ad give to tell you this?

_____

_____

_____

_____

_____

_____

In the box to the right, make an advertisement for an ice cream you might create.

Dangerous Substances

Read the following article. Answer the question that follows each paragraph to find the main idea.

1. Sometimes adults need to keep things in the house or garage that may be dangerous for children. Cleaners, paints, and medicines can be very useful, but they can also hurt or even kill young children. They should be used by adults only.

What is the writer telling you? _____

_____

_____

2. Containers that hold poisonous materials should be kept out of a child's reach. The containers should also have warning labels on them. A warning label is a sticker that has an illustration of a skull and crossbones on it. This is a symbol for DANGER. It tells kids to stay away.

What is the writer telling you? _____

_____

_____

3. It is a good idea for every family to check their own household for containers that hold dangerous materials. Parents can attach warning labels to these items and put them in places that children can't reach. These steps will provide every family member a safe and secure environment.

What is the writer telling you? _____

_____

_____

Try this: Create a warning label for a bottle of dangerous material. Make sure it tells why the bottle is dangerous.

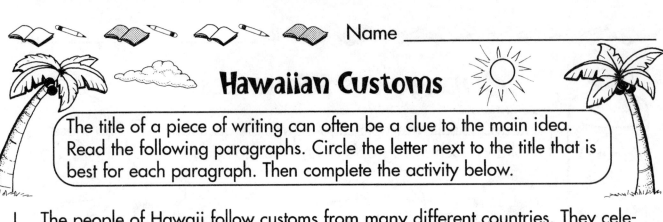

Name _____

Hawaiian Customs

The title of a piece of writing can often be a clue to the main idea. Read the following paragraphs. Circle the letter next to the title that is best for each paragraph. Then complete the activity below.

1. The people of Hawaii follow customs from many different countries. They celebrate American holidays like Thanksgiving with turkey. They take their shoes off at the front door of the house in the Japanese manner. They also enjoy Chinese foods and traditions.

   a. Chinese Traditions in Hawaii
   b. One People, Different Customs
   c. The Hawaiian Islands

2. Hawaiians often come together for traditional feasts. These feasts are called *luaus*. There is plenty of food at a luau. A pig and fish are roasted in an open pit in the ground, and taro stems are pounded into a paste to eat. People enjoy music and dancing at luaus, too. Luaus are an enjoyable Hawaiian tradition.

   a. Lots of Fun at Luaus
   b. Pigs and Fish—Yum!
   c. Hawaiian Traditions

Imagine you are on a trip to Hawaii! Write a postcard to your class. Describe some things you have seen and/or done on your vacation. On the back of your paper, draw the front side (picture side) of the postcard.

Postage Required

The President's House

The title of a piece of writing can often be a clue to the main idea. Read the following paragraphs. Circle the letter next to the title that is best for each paragraph.

1. After the United States became a country, its leaders wanted to build a permanent home for the president. The federal government announced a contest to design the president's house. Many architects and designers entered the contest. The winner was a man named James Hoban. Mr. Hoban was an Irish immigrant. He had only lived in America for about seven years, but his drawing of a three-story stone building was chosen as the best. The man from Ireland created one of America's most famous buildings.

A good title for this paragraph would be...

    a. An Irish Immigrant

    b. A Home for the President

    c. Entering the Contest!

2. The White House has had many changes since it was built. Modern conveniences such as running water, electricity, and elevators were added as they became available. Later, telephones, televisions, and computers were also introduced. Some features, such as a movie theater and bowling lanes, were added for entertainment. The White House continues to be updated, making the president's life easier and more enjoyable.

A good title for this paragraph would be...

    a. Inventions

    b. White House Entertainment

    c. The Changing White House

Try this: Imagine that you are the child of the president of the United States. Write a letter to a friend describing your home and your experiences.

Name That Book

Read each of the following book descriptions. Then, make up a title for each one. Write the titles on the book covers. Your titles can be silly or serious.

1. This book is for people who like warthogs, or are interested in knowing more about warthogs. It discusses their appearance, their habits, and their homes.

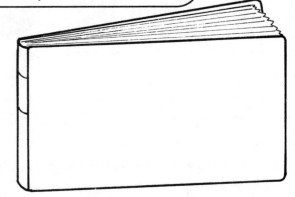

2. This book tells the story of a boy who is growing up in the inner city. His older sister belongs to a gang. His father tries to keep him from making the same mistake.

3. This book explains how houses are built. A construction worker shows the steps it takes to build a home.

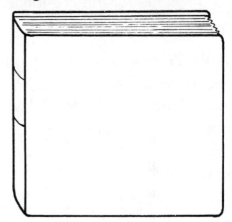

4. This book describes a day in the life of a circus clown. It tells what it is like to travel with the circus and to make people laugh.

Draw a picture on this cover, too!

What's on the Radio?

Read the following paragraphs. Then, place a check mark (✓) on the line that best tells the main idea of the paragraph.

1. When you turn on your radio, you may hear music, or you may hear a voice speaking. The person behind that voice is called an announcer. An announcer introduces songs, interviews guests, and gives news and weather reports. Beside spending time on the air talking, announcers also spend a lot of time off the air getting ready for their shows. That way, when the time comes for them to go on the air, they feel prepared and confident.

Which is the best example of the main idea?

____ You can hear music or voices when you turn on the radio.

____ Announcers get to talk to guests and introduce songs.

____ Announcers are people who talk on the radio.

2. There are thousands of radio stations operating around the world. Some of them play music most of the time. Rock and roll, classical, jazz, and country music are just some of the types of music that listeners can choose. More than ever, it is possible to find a radio station that plays what you like. Other radio stations are "talk radio" stations. They have people who discuss topics such as sports, politics, personal problems, and the news.

Which is the best example of the main idea?

____ Some radio stations are mostly "talk."

____ Radio stations offer many different choices to listeners.

____ Radio stations operate all over the world.

Check the type of radio station you like best. Circle the type of station your parents like best. Place an X on the type you think you would like the least.

rock and roll   country   classical   pop

sports   news   talk show

Name _____

Crazy Correspondence

Read the following letter. Cross out all the sentences that do not fit with the main idea. Then answer the questions.

Dear Dirk,

    I hope I won't hurt your feelings by saying that I have decided not to eat your cake. Although it is certainly lovely and large, I find the taste not to my liking. I had another cake last week that suited me just fine, despite it only being the size of my pencil tip. My reasons, you will find, are numerous. The flour that you have used comes from Xanadu and, since I am not a native, I cannot stomach its peculiar flavor. By the way, how did you ever manage to climb to the peak of Mount Lalawakas? You have used dried cherries and nuts, which, since I am from the upper east side, you know I cannot digest. Mother's indigestion has gotten even worse since the last wave of toxic wind. Father's was so bad before he left he could eat nothing but applesauce. Most importantly, because of my allergy to the South American killer bee, I cannot consume the honey topping without experiencing breathing difficulties.

    Please give my regards to all the animals, and let me know how your experimental toilet is working out.

                Sincerely,
                Sir Samuel Solomon

1. What is the main reason Sir Samuel doesn't like Dirk's cake?

_____

2. What specific reasons does he give for not liking it?

_____

_____

Try this: Write a letter in response from Dirk to Sir Samuel Solomon.

A Sparkling Morning

Read the following cereal box and answer the questions.

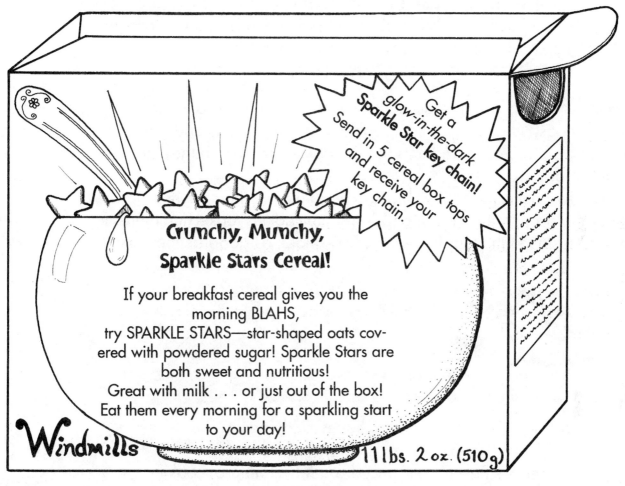

Get a glow-in-the-dark **Sparkle Star key chain!** Send in 5 cereal box tops and receive your key chain.

Crunchy, Munchy, Sparkle Stars Cereal!

If your breakfast cereal gives you the morning BLAHS,
try SPARKLE STARS—star-shaped oats covered with powdered sugar! Sparkle Stars are both sweet and nutritious!
Great with milk . . . or just out of the box!
Eat them every morning for a sparkling start to your day!

Windmills

11 lbs. 2 oz. (510 g)

1. What is the main reason you should buy Sparkle Stars cereal?

    a. They are covered with powdered sugar.
    b. Sparkle Stars will perk up your morning.
    c. They taste great with milk.

2. What details does the ad give to tell you this?

    _____

    _____

3. What can you get in addition to cereal? _____

    _____

Name _____

Henry's Cookies

In longer stories, each paragraph may be about the same topic but is about a different point. Therefore, each paragraph has a different main idea. Read the following selection and answer the questions.

Henry's Bakery just introduced a new cookie to its product line. Its ingredients include eggs, whole-wheat flour, baking powder, butter, and oats. Henry uses all natural, wholesome ingredients in this cookie. He adds honey and vanilla to make it taste good.

The new cookies weren't a big success at first. When the first batches came out of the oven, they smelled good, but the cookies looked uninteresting. So, Henry added raisins to the top. Now the cookies look as good as they taste!

What is the main idea of the first paragraph?

    a. Henry's cookies contain honey and vanilla.
    b. Henry uses all natural, healthy ingredients.
    c. Henry's Bakery introduced a new, all natural cookie.

What is the main idea of the second paragraph?

    a. Henry added raisins to the tops of his cookies.
    b. Henry had to make his cookies look more interesting.
    c. The cookies smelled good straight out of the oven.

Try this: Write a recipe for Henry's cookies, or for one of your own. Or, draw a sign to advertise Henry's cookies. Be sure to include the cookie's name, its price, and why people should try it.

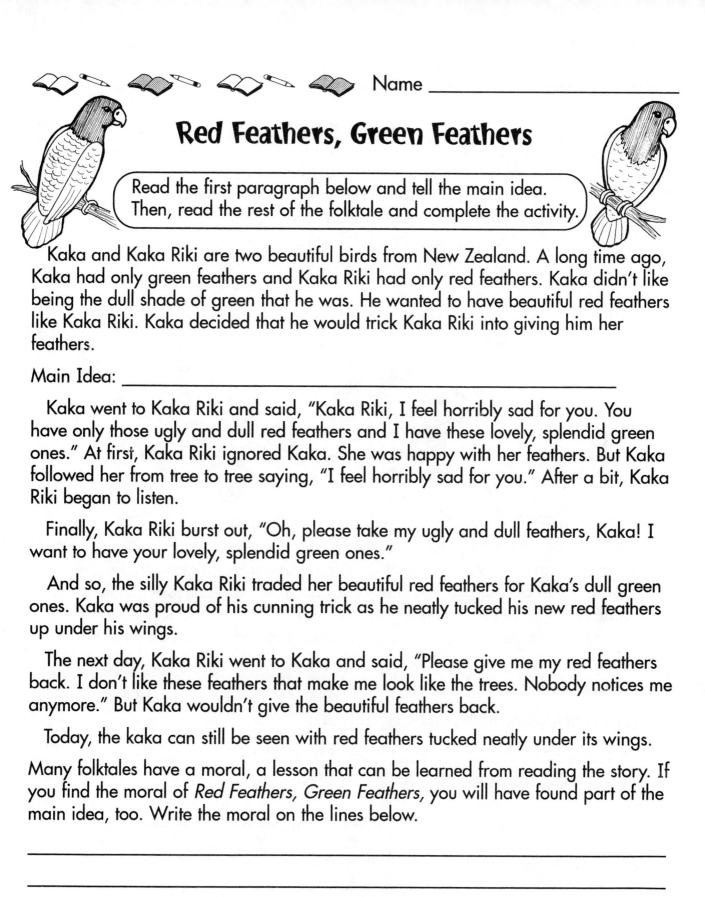

Red Feathers, Green Feathers

Read the first paragraph below and tell the main idea.
Then, read the rest of the folktale and complete the activity.

Kaka and Kaka Riki are two beautiful birds from New Zealand. A long time ago, Kaka had only green feathers and Kaka Riki had only red feathers. Kaka didn't like being the dull shade of green that he was. He wanted to have beautiful red feathers like Kaka Riki. Kaka decided that he would trick Kaka Riki into giving him her feathers.

Main Idea: _____

Kaka went to Kaka Riki and said, "Kaka Riki, I feel horribly sad for you. You have only those ugly and dull red feathers and I have these lovely, splendid green ones." At first, Kaka Riki ignored Kaka. She was happy with her feathers. But Kaka followed her from tree to tree saying, "I feel horribly sad for you." After a bit, Kaka Riki began to listen.

Finally, Kaka Riki burst out, "Oh, please take my ugly and dull feathers, Kaka! I want to have your lovely, splendid green ones."

And so, the silly Kaka Riki traded her beautiful red feathers for Kaka's dull green ones. Kaka was proud of his cunning trick as he neatly tucked his new red feathers up under his wings.

The next day, Kaka Riki went to Kaka and said, "Please give me my red feathers back. I don't like these feathers that make me look like the trees. Nobody notices me anymore." But Kaka wouldn't give the beautiful feathers back.

Today, the kaka can still be seen with red feathers tucked neatly under its wings.

Many folktales have a moral, a lesson that can be learned from reading the story. If you find the moral of *Red Feathers, Green Feathers,* you will have found part of the main idea, too. Write the moral on the lines below.

_____

_____

_____

_____

Families of All Kinds

Read the following paragraph, then answer the questions.

Remember: Find the topic by asking, "Who or what is this about?"

Find the main idea by asking, "What is the writer's point? What is the writer trying to tell me about the topic?"

The supporting details explain and support the main idea.

There are many different kinds of families. There are *nuclear* families— families with two parents and their children. *Single-parent* households consist of one parent and his or her children. When a mother or father remarries, the new family members become part of a *stepfamily*. There are also *extended* families—families with grandparents or other relatives living in the house. Still other families, such as *foster* families, are made up of people who care about each other even though they aren't related.

1. Who or what is this about? _____

2. What is the writer's point? _____

   _____

3. Give five supporting details.

   a. _____

   b. _____

   c. _____

   d. _____

   e. _____

16

A Very Special Olympics

A topic sentence can be found anywhere in a paragraph. It includes the topic of the paragraph. Supporting details are included throughout the paragraph to give more information.

Read the following article. The topic sentence has been underlined in each paragraph.

Every year, thousands of athletes meet in a different city. They compete in different sports to win medals. <u>This very special event is called the Special Olympics.</u>

<u>The athletes who participate in the Special Olympics are great athletes.</u> They train hard and test their limits. They work hard to win, but they know that winning isn't everything. They just have to try their best.

<u>The athletes of the Special Olympics are all mentally disabled.</u> This means that they do not learn as quickly or understand things as well as other people. This does not stop them from becoming Olympic champions!

Help this athlete ski to the bottom! Write supporting details in the blanks all the way to the finish line.

Athletes of the Special Olympics . . .

_____

_____

_____

_____

_____

_____

_____

_____

_____

Life in the Ballet

Read the following paragraphs and answer the questions.

1. Have you ever seen the ballet? The stage is filled with dancers in beautiful costumes. All ballet dancers train for hours every day. Dancing takes a lot of hard work and discipline. Discipline means exercising and practicing over and over again. By the end of the day, the dancers are tired and their feet hurt!

What is the topic? _____

What is the main idea?

a. Ballet dancers train very hard.

b. Ballet dancers have tired feet.

c. Ballet dancers get to wear beautiful costumes.

2. In the evening, after hours of class and rehearsal, it is time for the performance. The ballet dancers put on special makeup and fix their hair. They dress in their costumes. When all is ready, the theater lights dim, the stage lights come on, the curtain raises, the music starts, and the dancers begin the performance. The performance is the best part of being in the ballet. It makes all the hard work worthwhile!

What is the main idea?

a. The dancers begin the performance after the stage lights come up.

b. Dancers wear special hair and makeup.

c. The most exciting part of the ballet is the performance.

Try this: It takes discipline to accomplish a goal. What goal do you practice or train hard for? Write a few sentences about it.

Rules of the Road

Read the following selection and answer the questions. Then complete the activity below.

An officer from the local police department visited the Shaker Road School to give a talk on bicycle safety.

"Here are some basic rules to remember," the police officer said to the students in the audience. "Number one—always wear your bike helmet to help prevent head injuries. Number two—ride a bike that is the right size for you. Do not ride a bicycle that is too large or too small. An incorrect fit could cause an accident." The officer continued, "Make sure you ride in safe places. Don't ride on busy roads or after dark. And finally, make sure that you register your bike with the local police. That way, if your bike is stolen, we have a better chance of finding it."

The officer smiled at the children. "Remember—ride smart, ride safe, and have fun!"

1. What is the police officer talking about?

_____

2. What does the officer want the students to do? _____

_____

Create a poster that presents the rules of bicycle safety.

The Web

Read the paragraphs and complete the exercises.

1. Is your classroom or home hooked up to the Internet? If so, you have probably explored the World Wide Web! Some people call it "the Web" for short. The Web is a great way to get and share information. The Web uses pictures, sounds, and colors to make learning exciting.

Circle the correct topic.

    a. the Internet   c. the World Wide Web

    b. different kind of webs

Write the main idea of the paragraph.

_____

_____

2. A Web site is a place on the Internet that gives you information on one topic. Web sites can be about people, places, things, or ideas. They can give you new information, sell things, and explain things. You can learn about almost any topic by exploring Web sites. To go to a familiar Web site, you can type in its "address," and the site will come up. To find other sites, you may want to use a search "engine," which will find sites for you.

Circle the correct topic.

    a. Web sites   b. surfing the Internet   c. Web addresses

Write the main idea of the paragraph.

_____

_____

Try this: Create your own Web site! Choose a topic, write in words, and draw pictures to make it interesting. The topic of my Web site is: _____

  IF5631 *Main Idea*

Name _____

David Has Dyslexia

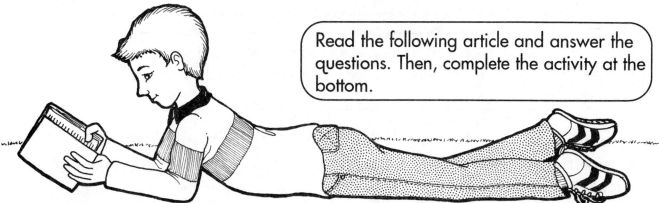

Read the following article and answer the questions. Then, complete the activity at the bottom.

David was having trouble in school. A doctor discovered that David had dyslexia. Dyslexia is a disability that causes problems with reading, writing, and moving. It is caused by the brain sending conflicting signals. Dyslexia makes learning more difficult. However, it does not mean that the dyslexic child is not intelligent. In fact, many people with dyslexia are very intelligent. They just have to learn how to deal with their disability.

When David first found out he had dyslexia, he was worried. He thought that he would have problems for the rest of his life. But, a teacher of kids with learning disabilities helped him a lot. David learned skills to help him cope and learn easier. His dyslexia is still a challenge for him, but he knows that it will not ruin his life.

1. What is the topic of the article? _____

2. The main idea of the first paragraph is _____

   _____

3. The main idea of the second paragraph is _____

   _____

Circle the word in the word pair that best fits the sentence.

People with dyslexia are not (stupid, smart). Most of them work very (little, hard) to overcome their difficulties. They are definitely not (lazy, happy)! If you know someone with dyslexia, maybe you can (discourage, encourage) them, and let them know that you will help them in any way you can if they need it!

Today's News

Read the news articles below. Then report on each article by writing the main idea on the lines below. See if you can tell the who, what, when, where, and why of each article in just a few sentences.

Terrible Tornado Torments

A huge tornado blew through Raging Falls, Michigan, yesterday at about 4:00 P.M. Residents and tourists were forced to flee to basements and shelters to wait out the storm. The City Hotel was hit hard when a huge tree crashed into the front lobby. The front of the building, which was all glass, was entirely destroyed. The lobby desk and all of the expensive furniture were swept out of the hotel by the tornado's powerful winds. Only one of the crystal chandeliers still hangs from the ceiling of the ballroom. Fortunately, no fatal injuries resulted.

_____
_____
_____
_____

Town Picnic Planned

The town of Raging Falls will sponsor a city-wide picnic on Saturday, June 28 to raise funds for the renovation of Playtime Park. The festivities will begin at 11:30 A.M. at the park and will last until 3:00 P.M. Activities will include Frisbee flying, softball, and volleyball. The playground will be available, and volunteers from the local daycare facility will be present to supervise children. Mayor Biggs will also be on hand to answer questions about the city's plans to renovate the park. The mayor will give a short speech and then lunch will be served. Please remember to bring your own plates and silverware. We hope everyone has a good time!

_____
_____
_____
_____

Name _____

The First Thanksgiving

Look at the illustration. Answer the questions based on the picture and on what you already know about the subject.

1. What event is taking place? _____

2. What is the main idea of this picture? _____

_____

3. How do you know what is happening and how the people feel?

_____

_____

Imagine that you are the dog in the picture. Write a paragraph describing what you see.

_____

_____

_____

_____

_____

_____

Arachna-Trivia

Read the following article. Write the topic sentence from each of the four paragraphs on the spider's legs. Then write the topic in the spider's mouth.

Many people think that spiders are insects, but they are not. Insects have six legs. Spiders have eight legs. Spiders are arachnids.

There are more than 30,000 species of spiders. There are house spiders and garden spiders. There are deadly spiders like the funnel-web. The jumping spider uses its short, strong legs to jump 40 times its body length. Others, like the water spider, swim under water.

Spiders are talented weavers who make beautiful webs of silk. The silk threads come out of *spinnerets*. The web is a spider's home, and it also helps the spider catch food. When an insect flies into the web, it gets trapped in the sticky threads. The insect becomes the spider's meal.

Spiders help control the number of insects in our world. Some people even keep them as pets. Spiders are creatures that are good for many things.

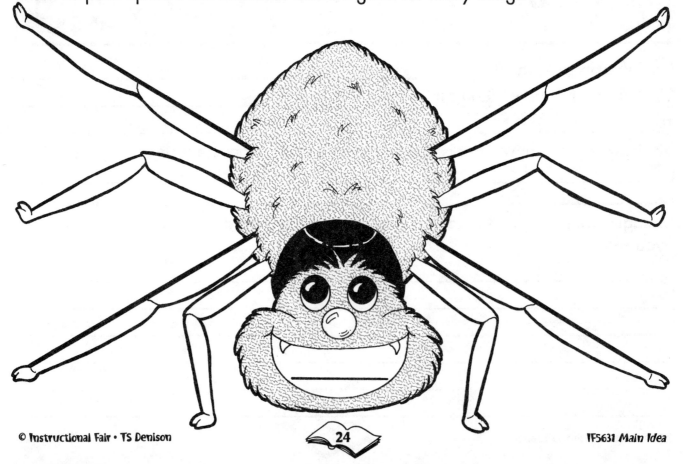

 Name _____

Early Colonies

Read the following paragraphs. Circle the word or words that show the topic. Underline the topic sentence.

1. In the year 1606, Captain John Smith began a settlement called Jamestown in what is now Virginia. Starting the colony was not easy. Smith's men were not used to the hard work of planting and farming. They almost starved. They came down with many illnesses. The Jamestown Colony struggled for a long time, but it became the first successful colony in America.

2. Before the Jamestown Colony was settled, a group of settlers landed on Roanoke Island near Virginia in 1585, but all of the men, women, and children disappeared! No one ever found out what happened to the people of Roanoke. The disappearance of the Roanoke settlers remains one of early America's great mysteries.

Be a reporter! Write a news story about the people of Roanoke. Answer some of the questions: Who? What? When? Where? Why? and How? You can add your own ideas about what happened to them.

The Colonial Times

Lead story: _____

Written by: _____

_____   _____
_____   _____
_____   _____
_____   _____
_____   _____
_____   _____
_____   _____
_____   _____
_____   _____

Name _____

Ocean Animals

> Read the following paragraphs. Circle the letter of the best topic sentence for each set of supporting details.

1. A fish's tail presses first to one side and then the other. The tail of a whale moves up and down. Eels, worms, and sea snakes move in an **S** pattern, bending their bodies. Scallops flap their shells, squeezing out water to push them along.

   a. The tail is an important part of a fish's body.

   b. Ocean animals swim in different ways.

   c. Animals crawl, run, and swim to get from place to place.

2. In order for most fish to swim near to the surface, they must do two things. They must move forward while trying not to sink. To control their buoyancy, fish must increase or decrease the amount of gas (such as oxygen) in their swim bladders. *Buoyancy* is the ability of an object to remain afloat in a liquid. Sharks, unlike other fish, do not have swim bladders, and must constantly swim to avoid sinking.

   a. Fish have bladders filled with gas.

   b. Most fish use their swim bladders to float in water.

   c. Sharks are unlike other fish.

3. Many people throw out their garbage without thinking about where it ends up. Often it is dumped in the ocean. The animals in the ocean try to eat garbage. Often they get sick or die. Turtles eat plastic bags. Fish and birds get tangled in soda can rings, and dolphins and seals choke on bottles.

   a. Trash is dangerous to ocean animals.

   b. Your garbage goes a long way.

   c. Sea animals get tangled up in plastic trash.

Action on the Set!

(Read the following story. Then complete the activity below.)

Max was visiting his uncle at work. Uncle Nate is a stuntman. He was working on a movie set the day that Max went to watch. The crew was filming an action scene. Max saw his uncle get in a "fight" with another actor. When the scene ended, the director yelled, "Cut!"

"That fight looked so real!" Max exclaimed. "When that man pulled a gun out and shot you, I felt kind of scared. Of course, I knew it was fake."

"We use fake bullets so no one gets hurt," Uncle Nate explained. "And, the blood from my wound is made out of honey with red dye added to it! The special-effects people work hard to make things appear realistic, but still make sure everyone stays safe."

"You have the best job," Max said.

"It is fun," Uncle Nate agreed. "But it is also hard work. I work long hours, and often we shoot the same scenes over and over again. It takes a lot of patience and experience."

"And a lot of laundry detergent," Max added, pointing to Uncle Nate's messy shirt.

A movie studio is hiring new stunt people! Write an advertisement that describes the job. Use supporting details from the story in your ad. Make sure it conveys the main idea of the job.

HELP WANTED!

_____
_____
_____
_____
_____
_____
_____
_____
_____
_____
_____
_____

Man's Best Friend

Read each paragraph and complete the activities.

Different dogs are used in different ways to help people. Some dogs are used by police. German shepherds can be used to sniff out illegal drugs or to track down and stop run-away criminals. Huskies are used to pull sleds in snowy regions. Other dogs help people who hunt by finding and retrieving game from the land or in the water. Sheepdogs, collies, and cattle dogs help farmers herd and drive sheep and cattle. Most importantly, all dogs make wonderful and loving companions!

1. What is the topic? _____

2. Write the main message of the paragraph. _____
_____

3. Circle the best title for this paragraph.

How Dogs Help People   Dogs   Dog Breeds and Their Characteristics

Some people with disabilities have dogs to help them in their everyday tasks. The dog is specially trained to assist blind or hearing-impaired people. Dogs chosen for these jobs must be smart and responsible. They must have good dispositions and be physically fit. Dogs that help the blind are called guide dogs or seeing-eye dogs. They help their owners walk down the sidewalk, cross roads, and go up and down steps and curbs. Hearing-impaired people use dogs called hearing dogs or hearing-ear dogs. These animals help the hearing-impaired become aware of ringing door-bells, telephones, cooking timers, and smoke detectors, as well as other household and street noises. Both seeing-eye dogs and hearing-ear dogs are useful animals and loving friends.

1. Topic: _____

2. What is the main piece of information you learn from this paragraph?
_____

3. What details support this? _____
_____

Name _____

Welcome to the Orchestra

Read the following piece of writing. Underline the topic sentence in each of the three paragraphs. Then complete the activity.

An orchestra is a group of musicians who play together on various instruments. The musicians' instruments are in the string, woodwind, brass, and percussion families. All these instruments come together to create beautiful music.

The viola, violin, cello, double bass, and harp belong to the string family. Some of the woodwind instruments are the flute, clarinet, piccolo, oboe, and bassoon. The brass family includes the trumpet, trombone, French horn, and tuba. The drums, triangle, xylophone, cymbals, and tambourine are examples of percussion instruments. All these families join to make the orchestra complete.

The orchestra is led by a conductor. The conductor makes sure that the musicians keep the beat and play the right notes. The conductor uses a stick called a baton that he or she waves in front of the orchestra to indicate the beat.

Write supporting details for each orchestra family in the notes.

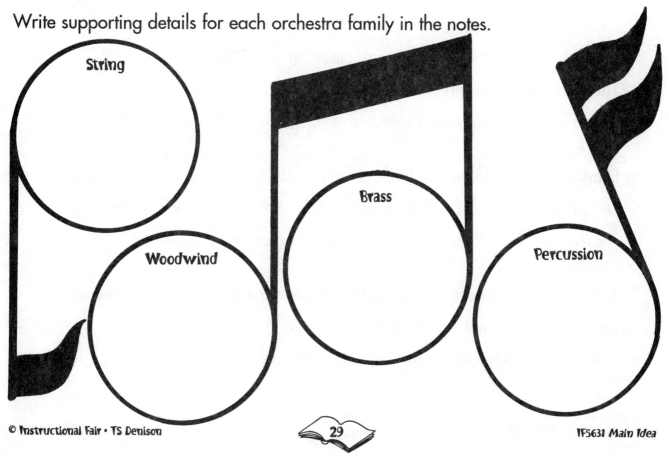

Life of a Princess

Read the list of supporting details. They are all about the same topic, but they support different topic sentences. Write the number of each supporting detail on the line under the topic sentence it fits best.

Topic sentences

Lady Diana Spencer grew up in a wealthy family.

_____ _____ _____

Diana became Prince Charles' wife in a fairy-tale wedding.

_____ _____ _____

Princess Diana's death was a shocking tragedy.

_____ _____ _____

1. The "wedding of the century" took place on July 29, 1981.

2. The Spencers had high social standing.

3. Diana wore a dress with a twenty-five-foot train and a dazzling tiara of diamonds.

4. Diana was only 36 years old when she died.

5. Diana's parents had a full-time staff to take care of their home and children.

6. The car she was riding in was traveling at a very high speed when it crashed in a tunnel.

7. The world was stunned when news of the terrible crash was reported.

8. Her childhood home was a mansion.

9. The prince and his new bride rode through the crowds in an open carriage.

Details, Details, Details

Read each of the following topic sentences. Write one supporting detail in each of the boxes for each sentence.

Many children like sports.

Sometimes it is good to turn off the television.

Try this: Write a paragraph using one of the groupings above. Add extra words to make it sound better.

31

Bill Gates, Computer Pioneer

Read the following story. Then answer the questions and complete the activity.

    Bill Gates is one of two men who formed Microsoft. Microsoft is the biggest computer software company ever. The company's mission is to put a computer on every desk and in every home. When Gates started his company, this seemed like an almost impossible dream. At that time, not many people owned computers or knew how to use them.

    Gates worked hard to make Microsoft a success. He put in long hours, seven days a week. His commitment paid off. Microsoft grew very quickly as people and businesses entered the "Computer Age." Gates became a billionaire in his thirties! Soon after, his company became the leading software company in the world. Bill Gates envisioned the future and has reached his goal.

What is the main idea of this story? _____

_____

The topic: Bill Gates

Three supporting details:

  1. _____

  2. _____

  3. _____

What is your favorite thing to do on a computer?

_____

_____

 Name _____

Survey Says . . .

A survey was taken of 100 third- and fourth- grade students—50 girls and 50 boys. They were asked what their favorite lunch foods were to see if there was a difference between what girls prefer and what boys prefer. Study the graph and answer the questions below.

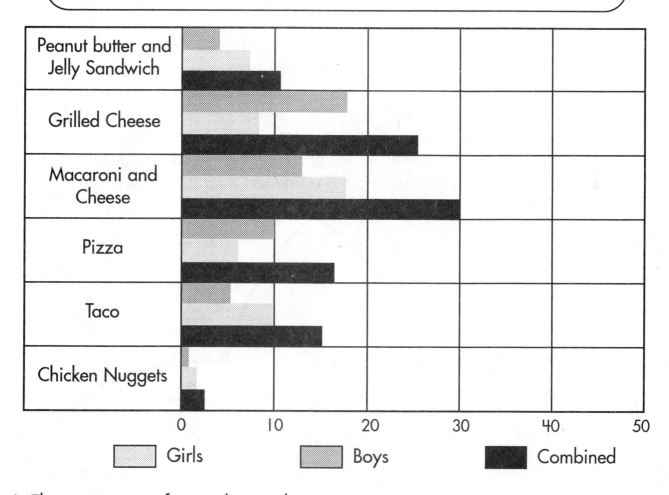

1. The main reason for conducting this survey is _____
_____.

2. What were the favorites for each group?   boys _____
   girls _____ combined _____

3. Did the survey accomplish what it set out to do? _____

4. Out of the choices surveyed, what would be your favorite lunch?
_____

A Sparkling Star

Read the following interview. Then complete the activity.

Annabel Sparkles was interviewed for an entertainment magazine. She was asked about her life as a movie actress.

"It's very exciting," the ten-year-old star of *Bubbles* confided. "I feel very lucky to be in the movies. But, it's important to know that it's not always easy being in show business. To be a good actress you must work hard and memorize all your lines. Even if you're in a bad mood you have to put that aside. You also don't get to be a normal kid. I don't go to a regular school. I get tutored on the set. I spend most of my time with adults who are actors, producers, and directors. Being in movies is fun, but sometimes I wish I were just an average kid."

Fill in the blanks of this sparkling star.

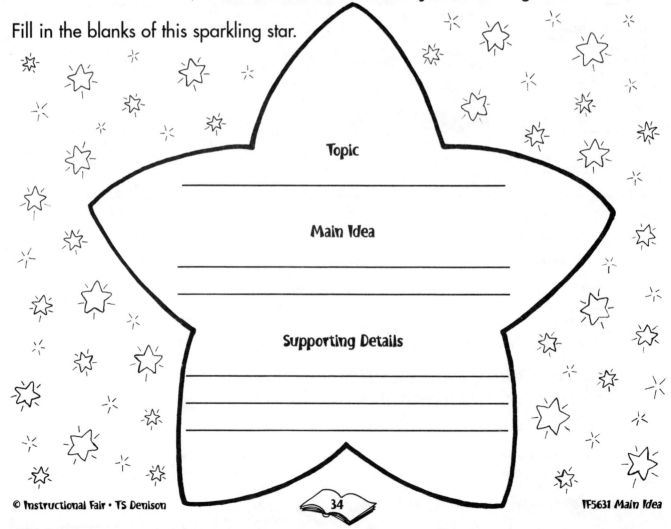

Topic

_____

Main Idea

_____

_____

Supporting Details

_____

_____

_____

Baseball Heroes

Read the following paragraphs and fill in each baseball card with the correct information.

Babe Ruth was a great baseball player who played for the New York Yankees. Many people believe that he was the best to ever play the game. He ranks second on the all-time home run list, with 714. He is first in walks, with 2,056. He ranks second in runs batted in (RBI's), with 2,211. In 1936, he was one of the original players to be named to the Baseball Hall of Fame. He is remembered as an American hero.

Babe Ruth

Why we remember him:_____

_____

All-Time Home Runs: _____   Team: _____

RBI's: _____ Walks: _____

Other accomplishment: _____

Mark McGwire is an American hero today. During the 1998 season he hit 70 home runs. This beat Roger Maris's long-standing record of 61. McGwire is fun to watch because he hits the ball so high and so far. He is known as a great power hitter . . . and a nice guy, too.

Mark McGwire

Why we remember him:_____

_____

1998 Season Home Runs: _____

Other reasons to like him: _____

_____

A Splendid House

Read the following Arabian rhyme and answer the questions below.

Little Girl

I will build you a house
If you do not cry
A house, little girl,
As tall as the sky.

I will build you a house
Of golden dates,
The freshest of all
For the steps and gates.

I will furnish the house
For you and for me,
With walnuts and hazels
Fresh from the tree.

I will build you a house,
And when it is done
I will roof it with grapes
To keep out the sun.

1. What is the speaker of this rhyme going to build? _____

2. Why will he build it? _____

_____

_____

3. Out of what four foods does the speaker say he will make this building?

_____   _____

_____   _____

Colors in the Sky

Read the following paragraph. Then fill in the rainbow arcs with supporting details from the story.

Look into the sky when the sun is shining behind you, and it is raining in front of you. You might be lucky enough to see a rainbow! Rainbows form when the sun's rays shine through raindrops. When the light passes through a raindrop, it bends. The light splits into seven colors. The colors of a rainbow are (from outside to inside): red, orange, yellow, green, blue, indigo, and violet.

Not all rainbows look like complete arcs. Sometimes you can see only part of the rainbow. No two people can see the same rainbow. Different raindrops contribute to different rainbows. You are always at the center of the rainbow that you see. For all people, however, rainbows are beautiful and colorful special effects in the sky.

Try this: Color the rainbow with crayons or colored pencils.

Chew, Chew

Read the following selection. Answer the questions after each paragraph.

Chewing gum is a popular treat. Americans buy almost two billion dollars worth of chewing gum every year. People around the world chew a lot of gum, too. Gum has been chewed in every place on earth from Africa to Antarctica. It has even been to outer space!

1. What is the topic? _____

2. What is the main idea? _____

3. Name two details that support this main idea.

_____

_____

Why do people like gum so much? There are many answers. Some people like its taste. Gum comes in many flavors. It also comes in many different shapes and sizes. Some people chew gum to freshen their breath, while others use it to clean their teeth. Still others say it helps them control their weight or stop smoking. Chewing gum can also be relaxing and help fight boredom. Gum is chewed for many reasons. What is yours?

1. What is the topic sentence? _____

2. Name some reasons people chew gum.

_____   _____

_____   _____

_____   _____

Try this: Write a poem about chewing gum.

Sent Out to Outer Space

Read the following paragraph and answer the questions. Then complete the activity below.

Space probes are spacecrafts that carry instruments into space. They travel to places people might not be able to. Space probes have gone around the sun and to planets millions of miles away. Equipment on board has collected data and pictures from places no person had ever seen. A recent Mars probe helped us learn many things about the soil, the weather, and the features of Mars. Many questions that scientists had about outer space have been answered with the help of space probes.

1. What is the topic? _____

2. What is the main idea? _____

_____

3. Write **T** (true) or **F** (false).

____ Space probes carry people into space.

____ Scientists have learned nothing from space probes.

____ Data from space probes gives us information about other countries.

____ Space probes go to other planets.

____ Probes carry instruments into space.

____ A probe brought back information about the weather on Mars.

Circle the names of the eight planets.

M	A	R	S	U	N	A	R	U
E	E	R	A	I	T	Z	I	E
R	C	I	T	P	L	U	T	O
C	Q	J	U	P	I	T	E	R
U	R	A	R	E	N	X	A	E
R	V	E	N	U	S	B	J	I
Y	Z	E	N	U	T	P	E	N

 Name _____

Review

Each of these groups contains a topic, a main idea, and three supporting details. Write the letter on the line that tells what each phrase or sentence is, using these abbreviations:

T = topic   M = main idea   S = supporting detail

1. ____ Children had moral books that taught them how to behave.
   ____ Children had school books that taught lessons.
   ____ Children in the olden days did not have many books to read.
   ____ Children's books
   ____ Children had to read adult books for pleasure.

2. ____ The English language has twenty-six letters.
   ____ The alphabet may be different in different languages.
   ____ The alphabet
   ____ An early alphabet, made up of symbols, developed in Syria.
   ____ The Chinese language has several thousand characters.

3. ____ Paperbacks are popular with book buyers.
   ____ Paperbacks are easier to carry around.
   ____ Paperbacks make up one-third of all books sold.
   ____ Paperbacks are cheaper than hardcovers.
   ____ Paperback books

Choose one of the above groups. Write a paragraph using the information given. Replace some nouns with pronouns and vary the sentences to make the paragraph sound better.

_____

_____

_____

_____

_____

_____

_____

Name _____

Review

Each of these groups contains a topic, a main idea, and three supporting details. Write the letter on the line that tells what each phrase or sentence is, using these abbreviations:

T = topic   M = main idea   S = supporting detail

1. _____ Over 100 nationalities are represented in Russia.
   _____ People in different areas of Russia speak different languages.
   _____ Russia is home to 150 million people!
   _____ The people of Russia
   _____ Russia is a country made up of many different people.

2. _____ Students of Russia
   _____ Russian students spend a lot of time in school.
   _____ Education is very important to Russian children.
   _____ Russian students who are talented go to special schools.
   _____ Russian students study math, languages, science, music, and sports.

3. _____ The first satellite
   _____ The name of the satellite was Sputnik I.
   _____ Sputnik I went around the earth once every 96 minutes.
   _____ The Space Age began when the Soviet Union sent up the first satellite.
   _____ Sputnik I was sent up in 1957.

Choose one of the above groups. Write a paragraph using the information given. Replace some nouns with pronouns and vary the sentences to make the paragraph sound better.

_____
_____
_____
_____
_____
_____

Answer Key
Main Idea—Grades 3–4

Mapping the Main Idea

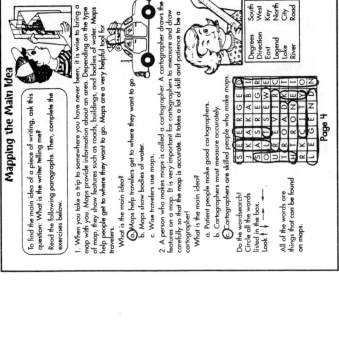

To find the main idea of a piece of writing, ask this question: **What is the writer telling me?**
Read the following paragraphs. Then, complete the exercises below.

1. When you take a trip to somewhere you have never been, it is wise to bring a map with you. Maps provide information about an area. Depending on the type of map, they show features such as roads, buildings, and bodies of water. Maps help people get to where they want to go. Maps are a very helpful tool for travelers.

What is the main idea?
- (a.) Maps help travelers get to where they want to go.
- b. Maps show bodies of water.
- c. Wise travelers use maps.

2. A person who makes maps is called a cartographer. A cartographer draws the features on a map. It is very important for cartographers to measure and draw carefully so that the map is accurate. It takes a lot of skill and patience to be a cartographer!

What is the main idea?
- a. Patient people make good cartographers.
- b. Cartographers must measure accurately.
- (c.) Cartographers are skilled people who make maps.

Do the wordsearch! Circle all the words listed in the box.
Look ↑ → ↓

S	E	V	E	R	G	E	D
J	K	A	K	A	B	I	I
S	A	S	R	E	G	R	R
O	U	R	E	V	I	T	E
T	R	O	A	D	K	T	C
H	R	O	N	E	I	O	T
R	K	C	I	T	Y	O	I
L	E	G	E	N	D	N	O

Degrees — South
Direction — West
East — Key
Legend — North
Lake — City
River — Road

All of the words are things that can be found on maps.

Page 4

What's the Main Idea?

Read each of the following paragraphs. Circle the letter that tells the main idea of each paragraph.

1. Reference books are resources that help you find information. There are a variety of references that contain specifics about almost everything you could imagine. You can find these books in libraries, bookstores, schools, and on-line.
- a. Libraries are good places to find reference books.
- b. Reference books come in a variety of forms.
- (c.) Reference books are good resources for information.

2. An almanac is one example of a reference book. Almanacs contain facts and information about a specific year. They describe events and tally statistics. If you want to know what happened during the year you were born, refer to the almanac for that year!
- (a.) Almanacs contain facts and information about a specific year.
- b. Almanacs show what happened the year you were born.
- c. Almanacs include descriptions of events and statistics.

3. Another type of reference book is a thesaurus. This book contains synonyms and antonyms. For example, if you want to know another word for *thin*, you might use a thesaurus. You will find synonyms such as *skinny* and *svelte*. The thesaurus will also show some opposite words such as *heavy* and *obese*.
- a. If you want another word for *thin*, you might use a thesaurus.
- (b.) A thesaurus is a reference book that contains synonyms and antonyms.
- c. A synonym for *skinny* is *thin*.

Try this: Look in an almanac for the year you were born! Find out interesting facts such as the number-one song, the president of the United States, and the best-selling book for that year.

Page 5

I Scream, You Scream!

Summer's almost here and the temp's gonna rise! So why not cool off with some refreshing, nutritious ice cream? Ice cream, you say? But of course. With Iditarod Ice Cream you get all of the vitamins found in a head of broccoli and more. Iditarod adds 100% of every vitamin and mineral to its mixture of cream and sugar. We also add all-natural flavors to make this ice cream the most refreshing and tasty. Not one preservative is added to our healthy creation. You won't regret making this positive life change!

Try some Iditarod Ice Cream today!

Comes in 40 fabulous flavors!

1. What is the main thing that makes this ice cream so special?
- a. has lots of vitamins.
- b. contains no preservatives.
- c. comes in 40 flavors.
- (d.) is refreshing and nutritious.

2. What examples does the ad give to tell you this?
100% of every vitamin
all-natural flavors
cream and sugar
no preservatives
comes in 40 flavors

In the box to the right, make an advertisement for an ice cream you might create.

Answers will vary.

Page 6

Dangerous Substances

Read the following article. Answer the question that follows each paragraph to find the main idea.

1. Sometimes adults need to keep things in the house or garage that may be dangerous for children. Cleaners, paints, and medicines can be very useful, but they can also hurt or even kill young children. They should be used by adults only.

What is the writer telling you? Dangerous substances should be handled only by adults.

2. Containers that hold poisonous materials should be kept out of a child's reach. The containers should also have warning labels on them. A warning label is a symbol for DANGER. It tells kids to stay away.

What is the writer telling you? Labels to warn children should be put on containers of poisonous materials.

3. It is a good idea for every family to check their own household for containers that hold dangerous materials. Parents can attach warning labels to these items and put them in places that children can't reach. These steps will provide every family member a safe and secure environment.

What is the writer telling you? By checking and labeling bottles, a home can be made safe.

Try this: Create a warning label for a bottle of dangerous material. Make sure it tells why the bottle is dangerous.

Page 7

Name That Book

Read each of the following book descriptions. Then, make up a title for each one. Write the titles on the book covers. Your titles can be silly or serious.

1. This book is for people who like warthogs, or are interested in knowing more about warthogs. It discusses their appearance, their habits, and their homes.

2. This book tells the story of a boy who is growing up in the inner city. His older sister belongs to a gang. His father tries to keep him from making the same mistake.

3. This book explains how houses are built. A construction worker shows the steps it takes to build a home.

   All answers will vary.

4. This book describes a day in the life of a circus clown. It tells what it is like to travel with the circus and to make people laugh.

   Draw a picture on this cover, too!

Page 10

The President's House

The title of a piece of writing can often be a clue to the main idea. Read the following paragraphs. Circle the letter next to the title that is best for each paragraph.

1. After the United States became a country, its leaders wanted to build a permanent home for the president. The federal government announced a contest to design the president's house. Many architects and designers entered the contest. The winner was a man named James Hoban. Mr. Hoban was an Irish immigrant. He had only lived in America for about seven years, but his drawing of a three-story stone building was chosen as the best. The man from Ireland created one of America's most famous buildings.

A good title for this paragraph would be...
   a. An Irish Immigrant
   b. A Home for the President
   c. Entering the Contest!

2. The White House has had many changes since it was built. Modern conveniences such as running water, electricity, and elevators were added as they became available. Later, telephones, televisions, and computers were also introduced. Some features, such as a movie theater and bowling lanes, were added for entertainment. The White House continues to be updated, making the president's life easier and more enjoyable.

A good title for this paragraph would be...
   a. Inventions
   b. White House Entertainment
   c. The Changing White House

Try this: Imagine that you are the child of the president of the United States. Write a letter to a friend describing your home and your experiences.

Page 9

Hawaiian Customs

The title of a piece of writing can often be a clue to the main idea. Read the following paragraphs. Circle the letter next to the title that is best for each paragraph. Then complete the activity below.

1. The people of Hawaii follow customs from many different countries. They celebrate American holidays like Thanksgiving with turkey. They take their shoes off at the front door of the house in the Japanese manner. They also enjoy Chinese foods and traditions.
   a. Chinese Traditions in Hawaii
   b. One People, Different Customs
   c. The Hawaiian Islands

2. Hawaiians often come together for traditional feasts. These feasts are called luaus. There is plenty of food at a luau. A pig and fish are roasted in an open pit in the ground, and taro stems are pounded into a paste to eat. People enjoy music and dancing at luaus, too. Luaus are an enjoyable Hawaiian tradition.
   a. Lots of Fun at Luaus
   b. Pigs and Fish—Yum!
   c. Hawaiian Traditions

Imagine you are on a trip to Hawaii. Write a postcard to your class. Describe some things you have seen and/or done on your vacation. On the back of your paper, draw the front side (picture side) of the postcard.

Answers will vary.

Page 8

A Sparkling Morning

Read the following cereal box and answer the questions.

Windmills

Get a
Glow-in-the-dark
Sparkle Star key chain!
Send in 5 cereal box tops
and receive your
key chain!

Crunchy, Munchy,
Sparkle Stars Cereal!

If your breakfast cereal gives you the morning BLAHS, try SPARKLE STARS—star-shaped oats covered with powdered sugar! Sparkle Stars are both sweet and nutritious!

Great with milk . . . or just out of the box! Eat them every morning for a sparkling start to your day!

1 lbs. 2 oz. (510g.)

1. What is the main reason you should buy Sparkle Stars cereal?
   a. They are covered with powdered sugar.
   b. Sparkle Stars will perk up your morning.
   c. They taste great with milk.

2. What details does the ad give to tell you this?
   Star-shaped, powdered sugar, sweet, nutritious, great plainer with milk

3. What can you get in addition to cereal?
   a Sparkle Star key chain

Page 13

Crazy Correspondence

Read the following letter. Cross out all the sentences that do not fit with the main idea. Then answer the questions.

Dear Dirk,

I hope I won't hurt your feelings by saying that I have decided not to eat your cake. Although it is certainly lovely and large, I find the taste not to my liking. ~~I had another cake last week that suited me just fine, despite it only being the size of my pencil tip.~~ My reasons, you will find, are numerous. The flour that you have used comes from Xanadu and, since I am not a native, I cannot stomach its peculiar flavor. ~~By the way, how did you ever manage to climb to the peak of Mount Kalawakaa?~~ You have used dried cherries and nuts, which, since I am from the upper east side, you know I cannot digest. ~~Mother's indigestion has gotten even worse since the last wave of hot wind. Father's was so bad before he left he could eat nothing but applesauce.~~ Most importantly, because of my allergy to the South American killer bee, I cannot consume the honey topping without experiencing breathing difficulties. ~~Please give my regards to all the animals, and let me know how your experiment todai is working out.~~

Sincerely,
Sir Samuel Solomon

1. What is the main reason Sir Samuel doesn't like Dirk's cake?
   He does not like the taste.

2. What specific reasons does he give for not liking it?
   The flour has a peculiar flavor.
   He cannot digest dried cherries and nuts.
   He is allergic to the honey topping.

Try this: Write a letter in response from Dirk to Sir Samuel Solomon.

Page 12

What's on the Radio?

Read the following paragraphs. Then, place a check mark (✓) on the line that best tells the main idea of the paragraph.

1. When you turn on your radio, you may hear music, or you may hear a voice speaking. The person behind that voice is called an announcer. An announcer introduces songs, interviews guests, and gives news and weather reports. Beside spending time on the air talking, announcers also spend a lot of time off the air getting ready for their shows. That way, when the time comes for them to go on the air, they feel prepared and confident.

Which is the best example of the main idea?
   ___ You can hear music or voices when you turn on the radio.
   ___ Announcers get to talk to guests and introduce songs.
   _✓_ Announcers are people who talk on the radio.

2. There are thousands of radio stations operating around the world. Some of them play music most of the time. Rock and roll, classical, jazz, and country music are just some of the types of music that listeners can choose. More than ever, it is possible to find a radio station that plays what you like. Other radio stations are "talk radio" stations. They have people who discuss topics such as sports, politics, personal problems, and the news.

Which is the best example of the main idea?
   _✓_ Some radio stations are mostly "talk."
   ___ Radio stations offer many different choices to listeners.
   ___ Radio stations operate all over the world.

Answers will vary.

Check the type of radio station you like best. Circle the type of station your parents like best. Place an X on the type you think you would like the least.

   rock and roll   classical   pop
   sports   country   news   talk show

Page 11

Families of All Kinds

Read the following paragraph, then answer the questions.
Remember: Find the topic by asking, "Who or what is this about?"
Find the main idea by asking, "What is the writer's point? What is the writer trying to tell me about the topic?"
The supporting details explain and support the main idea.

There are many different kinds of families. There are *nuclear families*—families with two parents and their children. *Single-parent* households consist of one parent and his or her children. When a mother or father remarries, the new family members become part of a *stepfamily*. There are also *extended families*—families with grandparents or other relatives living in the house. Still other families, such as foster families, are made up of people who care about each other even though they aren't related.

1. Who or what is this about? __families__
2. What is the writer's point? __There are many__ __different kinds of families.__
3. Give five supporting details.
   a. __nuclear families__
   b. __single-parent households__
   c. __stepfamilies__
   d. __extended families__
   e. __foster families__

Page 16

Rules of the Road

An officer from the local police department visited the Shaker Road School to give a talk on bicycle safety.

"Here are some basic rules to remember," the police officer said to the students in the audience. "Number one—always wear your bike helmet to help prevent head injuries. Number two—ride a bike that is the right size for you. Do not ride a bicycle that is too large or too small. An incorrect fit could cause an accident." The officer continued, "Make sure you ride in safe places. Don't ride on busy roads or after dark. And finally, make sure that you register your bike with the local police. That way, if your bike is stolen, we have a better chance of finding it."
The officer smiled at the children. "Remember—ride smart, ride safe, and have fun!"

1. What is the police officer talking about? __bicycle safety__
2. What does the officer want the students to do? __To remember basic__ __rules so they can ride safely and smartly__ __and have fun.__

Create a poster that presents the rules of bicycle safety.

1. Always wear a helmet.
2. Ride the correct size bike.
3. Ride in safe places.
4. Register your bike.

Page 19

Red Feathers, Green Feathers

Read the first paragraph below and tell the main idea. Then, read the rest of the folktale and complete the activity.

Kaka and Kaka Riki are two beautiful birds from New Zealand. A long time ago, Kaka had only green feathers and Kaka Riki had only red feathers. Kaka didn't like being the dull shade of green that he was. He wanted to have beautiful red feathers like Kaka Riki. Kaka decided that he would trick Kaka Riki into giving him her feathers.

Main Idea: __Kaka is jealous of Kaka Riki's feathers__ __and will trick her to get them.__

Kaka went to Kaka Riki and said, "Kaka Riki, I feel horribly sad for you. You have only those ugly and dull red feathers and I have these lovely, splendid green ones." At first, Kaka Riki ignored Kaka. She was happy with her feathers. But Kaka followed her from free to free saying, "I feel horribly sad for you." After a bit, Kaka Riki began to listen.

Finally, Kaka Riki burst out, "Oh, please take my ugly and dull red feathers, Kaka! I want to have your lovely, splendid green ones."

And so, the silly Kaka Riki traded her beautiful red feathers for Kaka's dull green ones. Kaka was proud of his cunning trick as he neatly tucked his new red feathers up under his wings.

The next day, Kaka Riki went to Kaka and said, "Please give me my red feathers back. I don't like these feathers that make me look like the trees. Nobody notices me anymore." But Kaka wouldn't give the beautiful feathers back.

Today, the kaka can still be seen with red feathers tucked neatly under its wings.

Many folktales have a moral, or lesson that can be learned from reading the story. If you find the moral of *Red Feathers, Green Feathers*, you will have found part of the main idea, too. Write the moral on the lines below.

__People and animals should be satisfied__ __with how they look. If they change, they__ __may regret it later.__

Page 15

Life in the Ballet

Read the following paragraphs and answer the questions.

1. Have you ever seen the ballet? The stage is filled with dancers in beautiful costumes. All ballet dancers train for hours every day. Dancing takes a lot of hard work and discipline. Discipline means exercising and practicing over and over again. By the end of the day, the dancers are tired and their feet hurt!
What is the topic? __ballet dancers__

What is the main idea?
(a.) Ballet dancers train very hard.
b. Ballet dancers have tired feet.
c. Ballet dancers get to wear beautiful costumes.

2. In the evening, after hours of class and rehearsal, it is time for the performance. The ballet dancers put on special makeup and fix their hair. They dress in their costumes. When all is ready, the theater lights dim, the stage lights come on, the curtain raises, the music starts, and the dancers begin the performance. The performance is the best part of being in the ballet. It makes all the hard work worthwhile!

What is the main idea?
a. The dancers begin the performance after the stage lights come up.
b. Dancers wear special hair and makeup.
(c.) The most exciting part of the ballet is the performance.

Page 18

Henry's Cookies

In longer stories, each paragraph may be about the same topic, but is about a different point. Therefore, each paragraph has a different main idea. Read the following selection and answer the questions.

Henry's Bakery just introduced a new cookie to its product line. Its ingredients include eggs, whole-wheat flour, baking powder, butter, and oats. Henry uses all natural, wholesome ingredients in this cookie. He adds honey and vanilla to make it taste good.

The new cookies weren't a big success at first. When the first batches came out of the oven, they smelled good, but the cookies looked uninteresting. So, Henry added raisins to the top. Now the cookies look as good as they taste!

What is the main idea of the first paragraph?
a. Henry's cookies contain honey and vanilla.
b. Henry uses all natural, healthy, ingredients.
(c.) Henry's Bakery introduced a new, all natural cookie.

What is the main idea of the second paragraph?
a. Henry added raisins to the tops of his cookies.
(b.) Henry had to make his cookies look more interesting.
c. The cookies smelled good straight out of the oven.

Try this: Write a recipe for Henry's cookies, or for one of your own. Or, draw a sign to advertise Henry's cookies. Be sure to include the cookie's name, its price, and why people should try it.

Page 14

A Very Special Olympics

A topic sentence can be found anywhere in a paragraph. It includes the topic of the paragraph. Supporting details are included throughout the paragraph to give more information.
Read the following article. The topic sentence has been underlined in each paragraph.

Every year, thousands of athletes meet in a different city. They compete in different sports to win medals. This very special event is called the Special Olympics.

The athletes who participate in the Special Olympics are great athletes. They train hard and test their limits. They work hard to win, but they know that winning isn't everything. They just have to try their best.

The athletes of the Special Olympics are all mentally disabled. This means that they do not learn as quickly or understand things as well as other people. This does not stop them from becoming Olympic champions!

Help this athlete ski to the bottom! Write supporting details in the blanks all the way to the finish line.

Athletes of the Special Olympics . . .
meet in a different city.
Compete to win medals.
are great athletes.
train hard.
test their limits.
work hard.
try their best.
at all mentally disabled.
do not learn as quickly.
are champions.

Page 17

The Web

Read the paragraphs and complete the exercises.

1. Is your classroom or home hooked up to the Internet? If so, you have probably explored the World Wide Web! Some people call it "the Web" for short. The Web is a great way to get and share information. The Web uses pictures, sounds, and colors to make learning exciting.

Circle the correct topic.

a. the Internet
b. different kind of webs
c. the World Wide Web

Write the main idea of the paragraph.
The Web uses pictures, sounds, and colors to provide information.

2. A Web site is a place on the Internet that gives you information on one topic. Web sites can be about people, places, things, or ideas. They can give you new information, sell things, and explain things. You can learn about almost any topic by exploring Web sites. To go to a familiar Web site, you may want to use a search "engine," which will find sites for you.

Circle the topic.

a. Web sites
b. surfing the Internet
c. Web addresses

Write the main idea of the paragraph.
Websites are places on the Internet that give information about specific topics.

Try this: Create your own Web site! Choose a topic, write in words, and draw pictures to make it interesting. The topic of my Web site is: _____

Page 20

David Has Dyslexia

Read the following article and answer the questions. Then, complete the activity at the bottom.

David was having trouble in school. A doctor discovered that David had dyslexia. Dyslexia is a disability that causes problems with reading, writing, and moving. It is caused by the brain sending conflicting signals. Dyslexia makes learning more difficult. However, it does not mean that the dyslexic child is not intelligent. In fact, many people with dyslexia are very intelligent. They just have to learn how to deal with their disability.

When David first found out he had dyslexia, he was worried. He thought that he would have problems for the rest of his life. But, a teacher of kids with learning disabilities helped him a lot. David learned skills to help him cope and learn easier. His dyslexia is still a challenge for him, but he knows that it will not ruin his life.

1. What is the topic of the article? __David__
2. The main idea of the first paragraph is __David discovered he had dyslexia, which causes reading problems.__
3. The main idea of the second paragraph is __David has learned to cope with the help of a teacher.__

Circle the word in the word pair that best fits the sentence.

People with dyslexia are not (stupid/smart). Most of them work very (little/hard) to overcome their difficulties. They are definitely not (lazy/happy)! If you know someone with dyslexia, maybe you can (discourage/encourage) them, and let them know that you will help them in any way you can if they need it!

Page 21

The First Thanksgiving

Look at the illustration. Answer the questions based on the picture and on what you already know about the subject.

1. What event is taking place? the first Thanksgiving.
2. What is the main idea of this picture? The pilgrims and the natives are cooperating.
3. How do you know what is happening and how the people feel? Smiling, both bringing food, their clothes, the turkey, the title of the exercise.

Imagine that you are the dog in the picture. Write a paragraph describing what you see.
Answers will vary.

Page 23

Today's News

Read the news articles below. Then report on each article by writing the main idea on the lines below. See if you can tell the who, what, when, where, and why of each article in just a few sentences.

Terrible Tornado Torments

A huge tornado blew through Raging Falls, Michigan, yesterday at about 4:00 P.M. Residents and tourists were forced to flee to basements and shelters to wait out the storm. The City Hotel was hit hard when a huge tree crashed into the front lobby. The front of the building, which was all glass, was destroyed. The lobby desk and all of the expensive furniture were swept out of the tornado's powerful winds. Only one of the crystal chandeliers still hangs from the ceiling of the ballroom. Fortunately, no fatal injuries resulted.

Answers will vary. The City Hotel's furniture and lobby were ruined when a huge tornado blew through Raging Falls at 4pm yesterday. No one was hurt.

Town Picnic Planned

The town of Raging Falls will sponsor a city-wide picnic on Saturday, June 28 to raise funds for the renovation of Playtime Park. The festivities will begin at 11:30 A.M. at the park and will last until 3:00 P.M. Activities will include Frisbee flying, softball, and volleyball. The playground will be available, and volunteers from the local daycare facility will be present to supervise children. Mayor Biggs will also be on hand to answer questions about the city's plans to renovate the park. The mayor will give a short speech and then lunch will be served. Please remember to bring your own plates and silverware. We hope everyone has a good time!

A picnic to raise funds for Playtime Park will occur on Saturday June 28 between 11:30am and 3:00pm at the Park. There will be food, activities, and a speech by the mayor.

Page 22

Arachna-Trivia

Read the following article. Write the topic sentence from each of the four paragraphs on the spider's legs. Then write the topic in the spider's mouth.

Many people think that spiders are insects, but they are not. Insects have six legs. Spiders have eight legs. Spiders are arachnids.

There are more than 30,000 species of spiders. There are house spiders and garden spiders. There are deadly spiders like the funnel-web. The jumping spider uses its short, strong legs to jump 40 times its body length. Others, like the water spider, swim under water.

Spiders are talented weavers who make beautiful webs of silk. The silk threads come out of spinnerets. The web is a spider's home, and it also helps the spider catch food. When an insect flies into the web, it gets trapped in the sticky threads. The insect becomes the spider's meal.

Spiders help control the number of insects in our world. Some people even keep them as pets. Spiders are creatures that are good for many things.

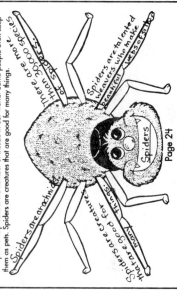

Spiders are arachnids.
There are 2000 more than 30,000 species.
Spiders are talented weavers who make beautiful websites.
Spiders are good for many things.
Spiders

Page 24

Early Colonies

Read the following paragraphs. Circle the word or words that show the topic. Underline the topic sentence.

1. In the year 1606, Captain John Smith began a settlement called Jamestown in what is now Virginia. Starting the colony was not easy. Smith's men were not used to the hard work of planting and farming. They almost starved. They came down with many illnesses. The Jamestown Colony struggled for a long time, but it became the first successful colony in America.

2. Before the Jamestown Colony was settled, a group of settlers landed on Roanoke Island near Virginia in 1585, but all of the men, women, and children disappeared! No one ever found out what happened to the people of Roanoke. The disappearance of the Roanoke settlers remains one of early America's great mysteries.

The Colonial Times

Be a reporter! Write a news story about the people of Roanoke. Answer some of the questions: Who? What? When? Where? Why? and How? You can add your own ideas about what happened to them.

Lead story: Answers will vary.
Written by: _____

Page 25

Man's Best Friend

(Read each paragraph and complete the activities.)

Different dogs are used in different ways to help people. Some dogs are used by police. German shepherds can be used to sniff out illegal drugs or to track down and stop run-away criminals. Huskies are used to pull sleds in snowy regions. Other dogs help people who hunt by finding and retrieving game from the land or in the water. Sheepdogs, collies, and cattle dogs help farmers herd and drive sheep and cattle. Most importantly, all dogs make wonderful and loving companions!

1. What is the topic? __dogs__

2. Write the main message of the paragraph. __Dogs are very helpful in many different ways.__

3. Circle the best title for this paragraph.

(How Dogs Help People)   Dogs   Dog Breeds and Their Characteristics

Some people with disabilities have dogs to help them in their everyday tasks. The dog is specially trained to assist blind or hearing-impaired people. Dogs chosen for these jobs must be smart and responsible. They must have good dispositions and be physically fit. Dogs that help the blind are called guide dogs or seeing-eye dogs. They help their owners walk down the sidewalk, cross roads, and go up and down steps and curbs. Hearing-impaired people use dogs called hearing dogs or hearing-ear dogs. These animals help the hearing-impaired become aware of ringing door bells, telephones, cooking timers, and smoke detectors, as well as other household and street noises. Both seeing-eye dogs and hearing-ear dogs are useful animals and loving friends.

1. Topic: __Specially trained dogs__

2. What is the main piece of information you learn from this paragraph? __Guide dogs are helpful and loving.__

3. What details support this? __Help owners cross roads, go up steps, hear phones, alarms, and door bells.__

Page 28

Details, Details, Details

(Read each of the following topic sentences. Write one supporting detail in each of the boxes for each sentence.)

__Answers will vary.__

(Many children like sports.)

(Sometimes it is good to turn off the television.)

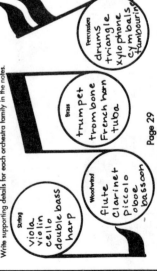

(Try this: Write a paragraph using one of the groupings above. Add extra words to make it sound better.)

Page 31

Action on the Set!

(Read the following story. Then complete the activity below.)

Max was visiting his uncle at work. Uncle Nate is a stuntman. He was working on a movie set the day that Max went to watch. The crew was filming an action scene. Max saw his uncle get in a "fight" with another actor. When the scene ended, the director yelled, "Cut!"

"That fight looked so real!" Max exclaimed. "When that man pulled a gun out and shot you, I felt kind of scared. Of course, I knew it was fake."

"We use fake bullets so no one gets hurt," Uncle Nate explained. "And, the blood from my wound is made out of honey with red dye added to it! The special effects people work hard to make things appear realistic, but still make sure everyone stays safe."

"You have the best job," Max said.

"It is fun," Uncle Nate agreed. "But it is also hard work. I work long hours, and often we shoot the same scenes over and over again. It takes a lot of patience and experience."

"And a lot of laundry detergent," Max added, pointing to Uncle Nate's messy shirt.

A movie studio is hiring new stunt people! Write an advertisement that describes the job. Use supporting details from the story in your ad. Make sure it conveys the main idea of the job.

HELP WANTED!

__Answers will vary.__

Page 27

Life of a Princess

(Read the list of supporting details. They are all about the same topic, but they support different topic sentences. Write the number of each supporting detail on the line under the topic sentence it fits best.)

Topic sentences

Lady Diana Spencer grew up in a wealthy family. __2 5 8__

Diana became Prince Charles' wife in a fairy-tale wedding. __1 3 9__

Princess Diana's death was a shocking tragedy. __4 6 7__

1. The "wedding of the century" took place on July 29, 1981.
2. The Spencers had high social standing.
3. Diana wore a dress with a twenty-five-foot train and a dazzling tiara of diamonds.
4. Diana was only 36 years old when she died.
5. Diana's parents had a full-time staff to take care of their home and children.
6. The car she was riding in was traveling at a very high speed when it crashed in a tunnel.
7. The world was stunned when news of the terrible crash was reported.
8. Her childhood home was a mansion.
9. The prince and his new bride rode through the crowds in an open carriage.

Page 30

Ocean Animals

(Read the following paragraphs. Circle the letter of the best topic sentence for each set of supporting details.)

1. A fish's tail presses first to one side and then the other. The tail of a whale moves up and down. Eels, worms, and sea snakes move in an S pattern, bending their bodies. Scallops flap their shells, squeezing out water to push them along.

   a. The tail is an important part of a fish's body.
   ⓑ. Ocean animals swim in different ways.
   c. Animals crawl, run, and swim to get from place to place.

2. In order for most fish to swim near to the surface, they must do two things. They must move forward while trying not to sink. To control their buoyancy, fish must increase or decrease the amount of gas (such as oxygen) in their swim bladders. *Buoyancy* is the ability of an object to remain afloat in a liquid. Sharks, unlike other fish, do not have swim bladders, and must constantly swim to avoid sinking.

   a. Fish have bladders filled with gas.
   ⓑ. Most fish use their swim bladders to float in water.
   c. Sharks are unlike other fish.

3. Many people throw out their garbage without thinking about where it ends up. Often it is dumped in the ocean. The animals in the ocean try to eat garbage. Often they get sick or die. Turtles eat plastic bags. Fish and birds get tangled in soda can rings, and dolphins and seals choke on bottles.

   ⓐ. Trash is dangerous to ocean animals.
   b. Your garbage goes a long way.
   c. Sea animals get tangled up in plastic trash.

Page 26

Welcome to the Orchestra

(Read the following piece of writing. Underline the topic sentence in each of the three paragraphs. Then complete the activity.)

An orchestra is a group of musicians who play together on various instruments. The musicians' instruments are in the string, woodwind, brass, and percussion families. All these instruments come together to create beautiful music.

The viola, violin, cello, double bass, and harp belong to the string family. Some of the woodwind instruments are the flute, clarinet, piccolo, oboe, and bassoon. The brass family includes the trumpet, trombone, French horn, and tuba. The drums, triangle, xylophone, cymbals, and tambourine are examples of percussion instruments. All these families join to make the orchestra complete.

The orchestra is led by a conductor. The conductor makes sure that the musicians keep the beat and play the right notes. The conductor uses a stick called a baton that he or she waves in front of the orchestra to indicate the beat.

Write supporting details for each orchestra family in the notes.

String: viola, violin, cello, double bass, harp

Woodwind: flute, clarinet, piccolo, oboe, bassoon

Brass: trumpet, trombone, French horn, tuba

Percussion: drums, triangle, xylophone, cymbals, tambourine

Page 29

Bill Gates, Computer Pioneer

Read the following story. Then answer the questions and complete the activity.

Bill Gates is one of two men who formed Microsoft. Microsoft is the biggest computer software company ever. The company's mission is to put a computer on every desk and in every home. When Gates started his company, this seemed like an almost impossible dream. At that time, not many people owned computers or knew how to use them.

Gates worked hard to make Microsoft a success. He put in long hours, seven days a week. His commitment paid off. Microsoft grew very quickly as people and businesses entered the "Computer Age." Gates became a billionaire in his thirties! Soon after, his company became the leading software company in the world. Bill Gates envisioned the future, and has reached his goal.

What is the main idea of this story? Bill Gates's company was Successful because he had a dream and worked hard.

The topic: Bill Gates

Three supporting details:
1. formed Microsoft / became a millionaire
2. worked hard / reached his goal
3. put in long hours

What is your favorite thing to do on a computer? Answers will vary.

Page 32

Survey Says . . .

Read the activity.

A survey was taken of 100 third- and fourth- grade students—50 girls and 50 boys. They were asked what their favorite lunch foods were to see if there was a difference between what girls prefer and what boys prefer. Study the graph and answer the questions below.

Legend: ☐ Girls   ■ Boys   ■ Combined

	0	10	20	30	40	50
Peanut butter and Jelly Sandwich						
Grilled Cheese						
Macaroni and Cheese						
Pizza						
Taco						
Chicken Nuggets						

1. The main reason for conducting this survey is to determine the different lunch preferences of boys and girls.
2. What were the favorites for each group? boys grilled cheese girls macaroni&cheese combined macaroni and cheese
3. Did the survey accomplish what it set out to do? Yes
4. Out of the choices surveyed, what would be your favorite lunch? Answers will vary.

Page 33

A Sparkling Star

Read the following interview. Then complete the activity.

Annabel Sparkles was interviewed for an entertainment magazine. She was asked about her life as a movie actress.

"It's very exciting," the ten-year-old star of Bubbles confided. "I feel very lucky to be in the movies. But, it's important to know that it's not always easy being in show business. To be a good actress you must work hard and memorize all your lines. Even if you're in a bad mood I don't go to a regular school. I get tutored on the set. I spend most of my time with adults who are actors, producers, and directors. Being in movies is fun, but sometimes I wish I were just on average kid."

Fill in the blanks of this sparkling star.

Topic: Annabel in the movies

Main Idea: It's not always easy being in show business.

Supporting Details:
memorize,no bad moods
don't get to be a kid, no
school,time with adults, Its

Page 34

Baseball Heroes

Read the following paragraphs and fill in each baseball card with the correct information.

Babe Ruth was a great baseball player who played for the New York Yankees. Many people believe that he was the best to ever play the game. He ranks second on the all-time home run list, with 714. He is first in walks, with 2,056. He ranks second in runs batted in (RBI's), with 2,211. In 1936, he was one of the original players to be named to the Baseball Hall of Fame. He is remembered as an American hero.

Babe Ruth
Why we remember him: He is an American hero who ranks second on the home run list.
All-Time Home Runs: 714   Team: NY Yankees
RBI's: 2,211   Walks: 2,056
Other accomplishment: 1936- Baseball Hall of Fame

Mark McGwire is an American hero today. During the 1998 season he hit 70 home runs. This beat Roger Maris's long-standing record of 61. McGwire is fun to watch because he hits the ball so high and so far. He is known as a great power hitter....

Mark McGwire
Why we remember him: He is a great power hitter who beat Roger Maris's record.
1998 Season Home Runs: 70
Other reasons to like him: hits the ball high and far, he is a nice guy.

Page 35

A Splendid House

Read the following Arabian rhyme and answer the questions below.

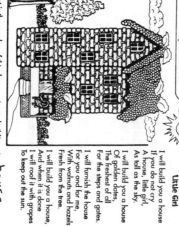

Little Girl

I will build you a house
If you do not cry,
A house, little girl,
As tall as the sky.
I will build you a house
Of golden dates,
The freshest of all
For the steps and gates.
I will furnish the house
For you and for me,
With walnuts and hazels
Fresh from the tree.
I will build you a house,
And when it is done
I will roof it with grapes
To keep out the sun.

1. What is the speaker of this rhyme going to build? a house
2. Why will he build it? He will build it so that the little girl will not cry.
3. Out of what four foods does the speaker say he will make this building? dates walnuts hazels grapes

Page 36

Colors in the Sky

Read the following paragraph. Then fill in the rainbow arcs with supporting details from the story.

Look into the sky when the sun is shining behind you, and it is raining in front of you. You might be lucky enough to see a rainbow! Rainbows form when the sun's rays shine through raindrops. When the light passes through a raindrop, it bends. The light splits into seven colors. The colors of a rainbow are (from outside to inside): red, orange, yellow, green, blue, indigo, and violet.

Not all rainbows look like complete arcs. Sometimes you can see only part of the rainbow. No two people can see the same rainbow. Different raindrops contribute to different rainbows. You are always at the center of the rainbow that you see. For all people, however, rainbows are beautiful and colorful special effects in the sky.

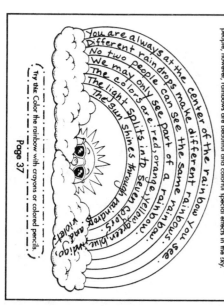

You are always at the center of the rainbow you see.
Different raindrops make different rainbows.
No two people can see part of a rainbow.
We may only see part of a rainbow.
The colors are: red, orange, yellow, green, blue, indigo, and violet.
The light splits into seven colors.
The sun shines through raindrops.

Try this: Color the rainbow with crayons or colored pencils.

Page 37

Chew, Chew

Page 38

Read the following selection. Answer the questions after each paragraph.

Chewing gum is a popular treat. Americans buy almost two billion dollars worth of chewing gum every year. People around the world chew a lot of gum, too. Gum has been chewed in every place on earth from Africa to Antarctica. It has even been chewed in outer space!

1. What is the topic? __Chewing gum__
2. What is the main idea? __Many people chew gum.__
3. Name two details that support this main idea.
__Gum is chewed all over, even in outerspace.__
__$2 billion worth sold in America.__

Why do people like to chew gum so much? There are many answers. Some people like its taste. Gum comes in many flavors. It also comes in many different shapes and sizes. Some people chew gum to freshen their breath, while others use it to clean their teeth. Still others say it helps them control their weight or stop smoking. Chewing gum can also be relaxing and help fight boredom. Gum is chewed for many reasons. What is yours?

1. What is the topic sentence? __Gum is chewed for many reasons.__
2. Name some reasons people chew gum.

taste / flavor	freshens breath
shape / size	cleans teeth
relaxing / fights	controls weight or
boredom	smoking

(Try this: Write a poem about chewing gum.)

Sent Out to Outer Space

Page 39

Read the following paragraph and answer the questions. Then complete the activity below.

Space probes are spacecrafts that carry instruments into space. They travel to places people might not be able to. Space probes have gone around the sun and to planets millions of miles away. Equipment on board has collected data and pictures from places no person had ever seen. A recent Mars probe helped us learn many things about the soil, the weather, and the features of Mars. Many questions that scientists had about outer space have been answered with the help of space probes.

1. What is the topic? __Space probes__
2. What is the main idea? __Space probes travel far away to study space.__
3. Write T (true) or F (false).

__F__ Space probes carry people into space.
__T__ Space probes go to other planets.
__F__ Scientists have learned nothing from space probes.
__T__ Probes carry instruments into space.
__T__ Data from space probes gives us information about other countries.
__T__ A probe brought back information about the weather on Mars.

Circle the names of the eight planets.

```
M A R S U N A R U
E   A I T Z I E
R R C P L U T O
C Q U A R E N X A
U R V E N B J I
R Y Z E N U T P E N
Y
```

Review

Page 40

Each of these groups contains a topic, a main idea, and three supporting details. Write the letter on the line that tells what each phrase or sentence is, using these abbreviations:

T = topic   M = main idea   S = supporting detail

1.
__S__ Children had moral books that taught them how to behave.
__M__ Children had school books that taught them lessons.
__T__ Children's books
__S__ Children in the olden days did not have many books to read.
__S__ Children had to read adult books for pleasure.

2.
__S__ The English language has twenty-six letters.
__M__ The alphabet
__T__ The alphabet may be different in different languages.
__S__ An early alphabet, made up of symbols, developed in Syria.
__S__ The Chinese language has several thousand characters.

3.
__M__ Paperbacks are popular with book buyers.
__S__ Paperbacks are easier to carry around.
__S__ Paperbacks make up one-third of all books sold.
__S__ Paperbacks are cheaper than hardcovers.
__T__ Paperback books

Choose one of the above groups. Write a paragraph using the information given. Replace some nouns with pronouns and vary the sentences to make the paragraph sound better.

__Answers will vary.__

Review

Page 41

Each of these groups contains a topic, a main idea, and three supporting details. Write the letter on the line that tells what each phrase or sentence is, using these abbreviations:

T = topic   M = main idea   S = supporting detail

1.
__S__ Over 100 nationalities are represented in Russia.
__S__ People in different areas of Russia speak different languages.
__M__ Russia is home to 150 million people!
__T__ The people of Russia
__S__ Russia is a country made up of many different people.

2.
__S__ Students of Russia
__S__ Russian students spend a lot of time in school.
__M__ Education is very important to Russian children.
__S__ Russian students who are talented go to special schools.
__T__ Russian students study math, languages, science, music, and sports.

3.
__T__ The first satellite
__S__ The name of the satellite was Sputnik I.
__M__ Sputnik I went around the earth once every 96 minutes.
__S__ The Space Age began when the Soviet Union sent up the first satellite.
__S__ Sputnik I was sent up in 1957.

Choose one of the above groups. Write a paragraph using the information given. Replace some nouns with pronouns and vary the sentences to make the paragraph sound better.

__Answers will vary.__